Cecilia McDowall

Everyday Wonders

The Girl from Aleppo

Upper voices, SATB, solo violin, and piano

VIOLIN PART

MUSIC DEPARTMENT

OXFORD
UNIVERSITY PRESS

SOLO VIOLIN

Commissioned by the National Children's Choir of Great Britain in celebration of its 20th anniversary

Everyday Wonders: The Girl from Aleppo

1. Orphans of the World

Kevin Crossley-Holland (b. 1941)

CECILIA McDOWALL

OXFORD UNIVERSITY PRESS, GREAT CLARENDON STREET, OXFORD OX2 6DP.

E

Meno mosso, expressive ♩ = *c.*80

144

mf

150

poco rit.

mf   *f*

F

Expressive ♩ = *c.*72

153

mf   *f*   *f*

159

mf   *f* *intense*

poco rit.

164

f

2. Thousands milling at the border
(The Journey)

TACET

3. I had never seen the sea before

attacca

4. A lost tribe pushed from border to border

attacca

5. *Everyday Wonders*

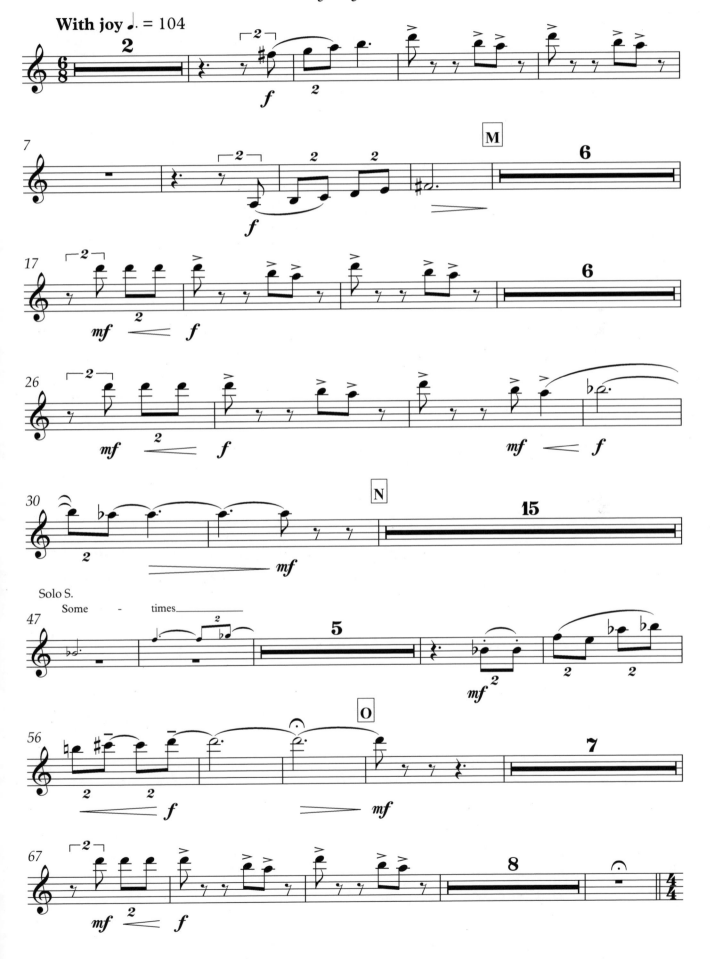

Expressive ♩ = *c.*72

f impassioned

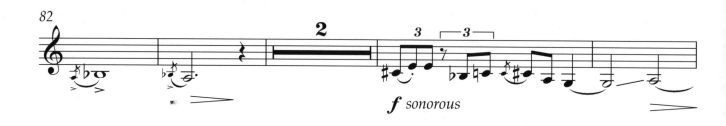

f sonorous

ritardando poco meno mosso ♩ = *c.*66

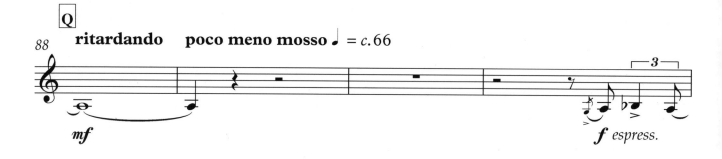

mf *f* espress.

f

mf *f*

ritardando

f *ff*